MOREL MUSHROOMS

Best-Kept Secrets Revealed

MICHAEL E. PHILLIPS

THUNDER BAY
PRESS
West Branch, MI

Morel Mushrooms: Best-Kept Secrets Revealed

Published by
Thunder Bay Press
West Branch, MI 48661
ISBN: 978-1-933272-31-3
Library of Congress Control Number: 2011946266

First Printing February 2012
Second Printing February 2019
23 22 21 20 19   2 3 4 5 6

Morel pen and ink drawing and illustrations of false morels © 2011 Shannon Weston Wood of Howell, MI.

Photographs taken by the author except where credited.

Thanks go to authors Phil Dickinson of Alanson, MI, and Anne Thurston of Boyne City, MI, for their help with editing. Thanks to Scott D. Cronin of Kalamazoo, MI, for computer help and guidance.

Book and cover design by Julie Taylor.

Printed in the United States of America.

In memory of my father

Franklin E. Phillips
who encouraged me to continue
working on my book

TABLE OF CONTENTS

PREFACE

I was first introduced to hunting morel mushrooms while I was a student at Alpena Community College. One of the classes I took was Dendrology (the study of trees) in the Forestry Technology field. The Dendrology program was taught in the fall and early winter while there were no leaves on the trees. Students were required to identify the trees by looking at the bark and twig/bud formations—all without the leaves. This program would become a major key in helping me find morel mushrooms.

In the spring of 1976, I was further introduced to morel mushroom hunting by the parents of Chris Weston (William and Betty Weston) in the Petoskey, Michigan, area. The very first morel mushrooms we found that weekend were the white/caramel colored mushrooms, which we found under dead elms, killed by the Dutch elm disease. After I figured out this connection, the mushrooms were easy to find because they grew large in this type of location.

After I moved back to my hometown of Battle Creek, Michigan, Chris and I remained great friends. While living in Battle Creek, I hooked up with other friends and was reacquainted to morel mushroom hunting with them while living on an island on Goguac Lake. Here I met former students from the Lakeview School District, Steve Morse and Richard Burdick. Richard and I would hunt morel mushrooms as often as we could get out.

While I was in the woods, I started to figure out which trees have an influence on where morel mushrooms come up. As I found these areas, I would write the locations and other notes down in a journal for future reference. With this information from the areas where I hunted and found mushrooms, I discovered that not all trees are characteristic with finding morel mushrooms.

In this book, I've collected the secrets I've learned for finding the elusive morel mushroom. I hope this book helps you become a successful morel mushroom hunter.

TYPES OF MOREL
MUSHROOMS

There are three different colored morel mushrooms: blacks, grays, and whites. All three colors have one interesting characteristic: they all have a honeycomb appearance. A perfect description of the morel mushroom's shape is that they look like tiny Christmas trees with a honeycomb texture.

The blacks are the first to come up and are usually smaller in size than the other colors, averaging 1" tall and ¾" thick at the beginning of the season. They will grow from 4-6" tall and 2-3" thick later in the season. Black morels are dark brown with black-brown coloring on the ribs of the honeycomb texture.

The gray morels are the second type to come up near the end of the black's season. At the beginning of their season, grays average 1" tall and ¾" thick. Later in the season they will grow 4-6" tall and 2-4" thick. The coloring of the gray morel mushrooms is quite interesting. The rib coloring is gray and the inner part of the honeycomb is dark black.

The last type of morel mushroom to come up is the white/caramel morel. Their whole honeycomb appearance is one color, French vanilla white. As white morels grow bigger, they start turning a caramel color and are thus called "caramels." Better known as white morels, these can get quite big as the season progresses, averaging in size from 6-8" tall and 2-6" thick, though they can grow bigger. The biggest one I remember was placed in a big shoe box with one end broken down. The mushroom measured 18-½" tall and 7" thick. The sheer weight of the mushroom crushed the stalk of that morel.

In the picture below, I have taken one of the white morels from the previous picture and sliced it into two pieces. Notice how the skirt of the morel is attached to the stem. This is the way all true morel mushrooms look when cut into two pieces.

TYPES OF FALSE MOREL
MUSHROOMS

There are four different kinds of false morel mushrooms that hunters need to be aware of:

1. Beefsteak, also known as Brown Brains, Globs, and Red Heads
2. Brown Bonnet
3. Elephant Ear, also known as Brown False
4. Yankee Cap, also known as Wrinkle Cap, Caps, or Half-Free Morel.

There are a lot of people who eat these and are not affected. However, I have heard of people doing strange things after eating these mushrooms, like stumbling and talking strangely with slurred speech. These false morels come up after the black season has started and end about halfway through the white season.

Beefsteak

The beefsteak false morel has a texture which is unmistakable. It looks similar to a brain with a rusty-brown color on top of a thick grainy stalk. These beefsteak morel mushrooms can get very big, about the size of a dinner plate. They start coming up shortly after the black morels have started and continue their growth well into the season of the whites. The beefsteak, if not prepared properly, can be very toxic.

Brown Bonnet

 The brown bonnet looks leafy with a brain-like texture sitting on top of a yellowish-white colored stalk (the stalk of the vegetable cauliflower is very similar). These can get a little bigger than a softball and can grow grouped together in large numbers.

Elephant Ear

The elephant ear is a brownish to caramel color, ear-like mass on an off-white/amber-colored stalk. These average 4–6" inches tall. I have only seen these on a few different occasions, and they are quite ugly.

Yankee Cap

    The Yankee Cap is a false morel with a unique texture and a wrinkly wavy cap. The skirt, or bottom edge of this cap, is not attached to the stem like true morel mushrooms are. The stem of this mushroom attaches on the underside of the cap at the top. The stem is unmistakable due to its light amber-white color on the outside, and the inside of the stalk has a white membrane all the way down the length of the stem.

CLOTHING

Whether you're hunting for a few hours or making an all-day trip, it's important to be dressed appropriately and have the necessary equipment and emergency supplies for traveling in the woods.

Having a rain suit that folds into a neat little packet, so it won't take up much space in your backpack, is also a good idea. Be sure to check the weather forecast before an all-day hunt and make preparations so you won't get soaking wet or cold.

You may also want to take a light jacket or a sweatshirt and maybe some extra socks. Put all clothing into sealable storage bags and compress them to get as much air out as possible. This helps conserve space in your backpack.

Sweatshirts

Wearing a short- or long-sleeved sweatshirt depends on personal preference as well as the weather conditions. I prefer a long-sleeved sweatshirt because I can push up the sleeves or quickly pull them down. Some of my sweatshirts are hooded for the cool days to help keep my neck warm. Cotton material is nice because it keeps sweat off the skin.

Pants

Long pants are an absolute must to keep your legs from getting cut or scraped. Blue jeans, corduroys, and khakis are the most common pants you'll see other morel hunters wearing.

Socks

Good, heavy, quality socks of either cotton or wool are the most comfortable.

Boots or Shoes

Wearing the right boots or shoes is important for the various types of terrains you'll encounter when morel hunting as you may be climbing up hills or stepping on or over logs or on slippery wet stones. I like a good quality boot with deep cleats for major hilly areas or a tennis shoe with deep cleats for areas of flat ground. Tennis shoes, later in the season, are good for keeping your feet cool. It's best to choose comfortable and sensible footwear for walking in the woods. Wearing dress heels in the woods is, obviously, not practical.

Jackets

Whatever type of jacket you choose depends greatly on the weather and personal preference. Choose a medium to heavy weight jacket for cool, wet, snowy weather. If the weather is cool in the morning and warms up as the day progresses, choose a jacket with a removable liner. You may even want to wear a raincoat to start, then take it off later and store it in your backpack if you have one with you.

Hats

Hats come in many different types, styles, and colors. Examples of various kinds of hats include baseball, straw, leather, cowboy, scarf, shawl, plastic, cloth, silk, fleece, bonnet, beach, etc. Whichever you choose, make sure it's comfortable. Hats help with maintaining body heat to keep you warm. They also protect from the sun, wind, and those nasty bugs that like to be a nuisance.

Gloves

On some days when you go into the woods, there may be a need to wear gloves due to cold, wet weather. You may want to wear gloves all the time if you have sensitive skin or allergies to various plants or soils.

Towel

I also pack a small hand towel to wipe away sweat or dry off after a brief rain shower.

EQUIPMENT

Having the proper equipment is essential for a successful mushroom hunt.

Plastic Vented Bags

First of all, consider taking plastic vented mesh bags you get from buying oranges, grapefruit, or onions in quantities of 5 – 15 pounds. The reason for using a plastic vented bag is to keep mold and rot away from your mushrooms. However, one problem with these bags is they will snag on brush and prickers. They can develop holes or even tear open causing your mushrooms to fall out. Nylon netted bags are less likely to do this.

Don't use paper or plastic bags because they will cause your mushrooms to mold and rot while you are out hunting. Non-vented bags make the mushrooms sweat quickly. Also, these types of bags will tear very easily, causing your mushrooms to fall to the ground.

On the right side of the following picture is my primary bag which features a shoulder sling. The top is made of cloth and the remainder is nylon mesh. The bags on the left include two orange bags and a nylon mesh bag with a draw string.

The orange bags are used for storage. They are also great for carrying through the woods, because you can get your fingers into the top few rows easily. You may want to keep others from finding out where your "honey holes" are located by keeping full bags in your backpack.

Backpacks

There are several different styles and sizes of manufactured backpacks. A school backpack is good enough for most mushroom hunters. I use a backpack which is a little more advanced. It has one water bottle on each side with cinch down straps, so when I am bending down to pick a mushroom, the water bottles don't fall out. There is a big compartment for storing empty mushroom bags as well as bags I have already filled. I always keep a quality rain suit folded in a pouch in that compartment. There are two smaller compartments to keep munchies and other miscellaneous items I may need.

There are two reasons for having a backpack with a big compartment:

1. To keep mushrooms from being crushed or broken from the weight of the morels at the top of the bag pushing down on the ones at the bottom. This happens from walking, stumbling, and falling on them.
2. To hide a big morel collection from other people who are in the woods so they can't see how well you are doing.

The backpack size depends on your needs. If you are going for a quick hunt, then you might not want to take a backpack. However, I have done this and then not had an extra bag with me when I found more mushrooms than expected. Or, occasionally I change my mind, turning a short hunt into a long hunt. Usually on an early season hunt, I won't take my backpack, but I always take an extra bag, a compass or GPS, and a water bottle.

Food and Water

When you are out in the woods hunting, you may start to get hungry. How much food to take really depends on you and how long you intend to stay out hunting.

For all-day hunting, food is a must to keep energy levels up and not let fatigue set in. The most common type of food I keep with me is trail mix made of seedless fruits, peanuts or cashews, raisins, and M&Ms. Another kind of food I keep in the backpack is my homemade jerky or store bought brands. Then there is always the old standby—candy bars. Keep in mind, they will melt if they get warm. Last, but not forgotten, are sandwiches. Peanut butter and jam sandwiches work well, but meat sandwiches may spoil on a long hot day.

It is very important to have some bottles or other containers with you for water or another type of beverage. A person can become dehydrated when spending a lot of time walking around in the woods.

Two types of beverage containers that I prefer are either plastic or aluminum containers with a screw-on lid or a flip-up top.

On my backpack I carry two containers of water, one on each side. The night before an all day hunt, I fill up my water containers and put them in the freezer. Then, before I leave, I put the bottles in my backpack pockets and the water does not warm up too fast. I make sure they are cinched into the pockets.

Never take glass bottles into the woods. They are heavy and there is always the possibility of breaking them. Then what would you do with a broken bottle? If you already had bag of mushrooms in your backpack, you wouldn't want to put a broken bottle in with the mushrooms. I hope you wouldn't leave the broken glass littered in the woods.

Compass and GPS unit

With the new technology of GPS units, you may choose to have a compass and a GPS unit with you. I usually carry two or three compasses with me. The reason I carry more than one is because I have lost at least four of them in my 35 years of hunting mushrooms, or I have broken them when I have tripped and fallen on a log or a stone.

With the new smaller sizes available for GPS units, I carry three devices: two compasses and a GPS unit with fully-charged backup batteries. Always keep extra batteries in a separate bag for the GPS. Carry an overview map of the area you are morel hunting. That way, if your battery dies while you are in the woods, you have a backup plan to return safely. If you cannot afford a GPS unit, carry a small notepad and keep it in a watertight bag.

Maps and Map Books

Maps and map books are great to keep in your vehicle, with a detailed copy of the area you are hunting.

When morel hunting in unfamiliar woods, I keep a blown up map of that township and sections in case I get turned around. Pens and pencils are a must to mark areas on the map so I can find them later. I can go to the map and make some kind of a symbol to identify that location. You may want to carry a pair of reading glasses for seeing the small print on the maps.

The most common map book I use is a State County Map Book. These maps have a total breakdown of highways, paved roads, dirt roads, railroad tracks, rivers, streams, lakes, foot paths, private lands, state lands, townships, and federal lands. This book is especially handy while I am hunting mushrooms, because if I find a new area with morels, I can make a small notation on the map and write down the GPS coordinates. I use a color code to keep the GPS codes separated from each other. I go one step further and write the location into a "log book" or "mushroom diary" and describe what I've discovered in that area.

Sometimes, depending on how serious you want to be in hunting locations, you may want to have a "Plat Book" of the area. On this you can mark the exact location if, on a later date, you want to return to the same spot.

Landmarks are another great resource to find your way out of strange woods (note such landmarks on your maps with other reference points). Examples include big rocks, unusual land formations, different types of trees, buildings, lakes, streams, rivers, etc.

The Buddy System

Having someone else in the woods with you is ideal, especially when searching a new area. You can usually stay in the same area or at least be able to hear each other.

If you have a buddy and something happens to either of you, the other person can provide assistance. Here's an example: one of my hunting partners has an allergy to bees, wasps, and hornets. If it were ever necessary to give him an allergy injection, I could do it and then get him to a hospital as quickly as possible for further treatment. If you decide to hunt with a buddy, let your partner know if you have any health concerns. Also, ask if you should be aware of any health issues your buddy may have.

Something else you and your buddy may want to have is a set of Walkie-Talkies with an extra set of batteries and whistles. Both of you should have a compass or a GPS unit (or both) in case you get split up.

Mushroom Guide Books or Flip Card Photos

It is important to know exactly what you are looking for. If you have never hunted morel mushrooms before and cannot find anyone to hunt with, take some pictures of the type of mushrooms that you are seeking. Most people who are hunters of this type of mushroom are very secretive of their hot spots. People won't even tell their own spouses or family members because they've found these areas and want to keep all of the mushrooms to themselves. I used to be this way. I'd find a hot spot loaded with mushrooms and I would reap all of the rewards for myself and not tell anyone. If other people wanted to know where I had been, I would simply tell them that I was in the woods. I wanted to keep certain areas a secret.

First-Aid Kits

Make sure your first-aid kit is complete with bandages and ointments. Check to see if any supplies are outdated.

Bee Sting, Snake Bite, or Hazardous Insect Kits

Depending on the geographical zone you're hunting, having a snakebite or hazardous insect kit may be something very useful to have in your backpack. Anyone with severe reactions should already have a bee sting kit with him or her. Know what hazards are in the area where you are hunting.

Lip Balm or Chap Stick

Lip balm and chap stick are not required, but individuals may decide whether it will be helpful. It may be important to protect your lips from the sun and wind.

Walking Sticks

When you are hunting mushrooms, it is nice to have a walking stick with you, whether it is a cane, staff, or broken branch. The sticks give balance when walking on uneven or slippery terrain and can be used to move undergrowth to uncover mushrooms that may be hidden from view.

If I come into an area that is loaded with mushrooms, the stick comes in handy to move leaves and small branches that are raised up, so I can see if there are any mushrooms hidden underneath. Checking the area with the stick is helpful because otherwise I might step on or destroy the mushrooms. My stick is about 5' long and is very strong. A carved morel mushroom decorates its top.

Bug Spray

Bug spray is a must, unless you are one of the lucky few that flies and mosquitoes don't bother. Some of these sprays will even keep the deer ticks off you. Another tip to help control the tick is to duct tape around the bottom of your pants, but don't wrap it so tight that it cuts off circulation. If the ticks find any bare skin, they will bury themselves and can make you very sick.

Rain Gear

Sometimes the weather is good, but other times you may have the threat of rain. It is a good idea to take a rain coat and rain pants with you, packed as small as possible into the backpack's large compartment.

Pocket Knife

I carry a pocket knife when I'm morel hunting. There are many uses for a pocket knife. This is one item I would never be without.

Cell Phone

If you have a cell phone, it's a good idea to take it with you when hunting. It can come in handy if you have an emergency or become lost. Keep your cell phone fully charged and store important phone numbers in it.

Flashlight

You can never tell how long you are going to be out hunting if the hunting is really good. The sun sets quickly and it may get dark before you realize it. Even if you know exactly where you are, a flashlight will help you to keep from stumbling, tripping, and hurting yourself. Always have extra batteries handy.

Camera

I like bringing a camera to take pictures of unusual places where mushrooms will grow. I also like taking pictures of large clusters of morels.

Maybe you will get really lucky while morel hunting and walk up on a newborn fawn. This is wonderful for a picture, because most people will not believe you. It's especially good if your camera is equipped with a date and time feature. If you do see a newborn fawn, don't touch it. Touching a fawn can cause the mother to abandon it. Enjoy nature while mushrooming, but respect it.

Matches/ Space Blanket

If you get lost, before you panic yourself into a frenzy, sit down and try to sort out where you are. If you are cold, you may have to build a small fire to get warm. Take all of the necessary precautions when building a fire in the woods and clean out a good-sized area to prevent the fire from spreading.

A space blanket is good for several reasons.

1. It'll help you stay warm.
2. It'll protect you from a spreading fire.
3. If you are really lost and people are looking for you from the air, the reflective side will help them spot you more easily.

Hot Packs

Hot packs come in handy if you happen to get wet or cold. When you open one, it gets hot and stays that way for a long time. In cool weather these items can make your outing more comfortable and enjoyable.

Litter

Usually while I am hunting, I will pick up any litter I find. I try to be a steward of the land and leave it better than I found it.

BACKPACK CHECKLIST

Backpacks are necessary for the serious hunter who starts out early in the morning and hunts mushrooms most of the day. The backpack is taken into the hunting area with extra supplies to make the hunt safer and more pleasurable.

The picture below shows a few of the items that I keep in my bag.

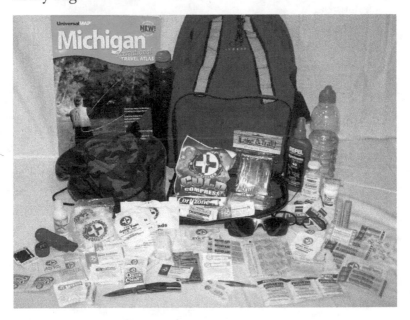

Items in my backpack

There are many different backpack styles which can be purchased. Keep in mind the stuff you put inside are the items you may need throughout the day. Purchase one big enough to meet your needs.

The following is a list of the items I carry in my backpack:

Extra meshed bags

◊ Plastic meshed (orange bags or onion sacks)
◊ Nylon meshed

First-Aid Kits

◊ First-Aid ointment
◊ Miscellaneous bandages
◊ Cortisone cream and hand lotion
◊ Aspirin or similar pain reliever
◊ Lip balm
◊ Antacids (Rolaids®, Tums®)
◊ Sun block
◊ Bug sprays
◊ Poison ivy relief
◊ Peroxide spray or packets
◊ First-aid tape

Maps and compasses

◊ Map book of the area
◊ Compass
◊ Pens and/or pencils
◊ Note pad (kept in a plastic, sealable bag)
◊ Reading glasses and sun glasses
◊ Lens cleaner packets

Food and Water

◊ Water bottles
◊ Food
  ◊ Cookies
  ◊ Jerky
  ◊ Candy bars
  ◊ Sandwiches
  ◊ Trail mix
  ◊ Nuts

Miscellaneous clothing

◊ Hats
◊ Rain suit
◊ Sweat shirt
◊ Light jacket

Miscellaneous other items

◊ Matches
◊ Whistle
◊ Cell phone
◊ Hand-held communication radios
◊ Batteries
◊ Camera
◊ Knife

GETTING STARTED

In this section I will cover the secrets of finding morel mushrooms and the descriptions of what they look like. As the season begins, there are some things you'll want to keep track of. First, watch the shrub known as the Forsythia bush. This shrub is primarily used in landscape design, and the flowers appear before the leaves. The flowers are a bright yellow color; there are four petals per flower, joined at the center. The bark on the branches of the Forsythia have an odd coloring. The new branches are amber-brown, and the older branches are gray-brown. Forsythias bushes grow on an average from three to nine feet tall and, rarely, up to eighteen feet tall. About a week after the flowers appear on this shrub, the morel mushroom season begins.

Another very good indicator of the start of the morel mushroom season is a North American weed known as the Dandelion. The flower has many bright yellow petals joined at the center. The base has deeply serrated leaves sometimes used in salads. When they first appear, the sheer number is an indicator to the quantity of morel mushrooms which may grow for the season. For example, in the spring of 2011 there were scores of dandelions growing everywhere and this was true for the morels also. We found morels growing in areas where we very seldom find them.

Warm days and nights (40s to low 60s is an ideal temperature range) with an adequate amount of rain (and in some cases snow) and humidity are all very important weather indicators to be aware of when hunting the morel mushroom. The right weather and damp soil are the main conditions needed to have a successful hunting season.

There are two types of soils in which I have never found any morel mushrooms: various types of clay (red clay, marl clay, etc.) and soils that remain wet all the time. The second type of soil is extremely wet and has a sandy feeling with a dark brown to a black color (swamp muck).

When the morel mushrooms start, the blacks (or dark brown ones) are first, next to come along are the grays, and then the whites (or caramels), in that order. There are other types of mushrooms that come up during the same time frame that often indicate excellent areas to look for the morel mushrooms.

This picture shows the texture of the morel mushroom "Honeycomb" look.

Depending on your geographic location, usually you will start to find the blacks near the ash, apple, poplar (also known as aspen), beech, oaks, common choke cherry, dogwoods, and maples. When the blacks are coming up through the leaves or grasses, you will need to look on the north and east sides of the trees, this is especially true around the ash trees. Most of the mushrooms that I find are in very hilly terrain, and most of the time they are found on the north and east facing hills. When they start to come up, look near the top or crest of these hills. After they have been coming up for a few days, start looking farther down the hills in the valleys where most of the rain fall or snow runoff will go. You will want to be looking around logs, branches, rocks, and in the leaves and grasses for them.

Earlier I mentioned that you may find other types of mushrooms in these same areas with the morel mushrooms. These are not what you want to pick and eat—ever. This is an odd looking mushroom that looks like a cup on the ground. They are seen in three colors: black, red, and tan.

Black Cup

Red Cup

Tan Cup

Normal looking types of toadstool mushrooms and lichen moss are other good indicators that the morel may grow in the area. If you are lucky to have vines growing wildly in the woods, this is a great place to find the mushrooms. As the season moves along, there are other areas to look for morel mushrooms, like stands of poplar trees.

Toadstool mushrooms

As the season progresses, the black morels come to an end and the gray morels gain prominence. The best shrub to watch is the lilac which blossoms in a range of colors from white to purple and red. The gray morels start to appear before the lilacs produce their flowers but after the shrub is covered with leaves. The gray morel's honeycomb texture has gray ridges and darker holes. These will get fairly large, averaging anywhere from 6-8" tall and 2-3" thick. I have not found very many of these. When I do get lucky, I look around the ash trees, poplar trees, fruit trees, and areas with rocks and downed timber. I have also found them growing near freshly cut tree stumps of red and white oak, red and white elm, ash, and poplars.

Tiny Gray Morel

Lilac blossoms

When the lilacs flowers start to appear, the white morels have started. If left alone, the white morels will turn a caramel color in a relatively short time frame. These will continue to grow and get quite big. Shortly after the lilac flowers have finished blooming, the morel season comes to an end, although some of the straggler whites have been found well after the lilacs quit flowering, even into the middle of July.

As the early spring flowers begin to bloom, there are several types seen with morels. Trillium, columbine, skunk cabbage, leaks (wild onions), lilies of the valley, dandelions, violets, dogwood tree flowers, lilacs, forsythias, etc. Trillium and columbine are shown below.

Trillium

Columbine

The white morel mushrooms are the most popular to hunt. These can be found in many of the same areas as the blacks: mixed hardwoods of ash, maples, beech, dogwoods, individual poplar trees to stands of poplars or aspens, red and white oaks, common choke cherry, fruit trees, elms (especially recently dead red elms), deep grasses and weeds, ferns, myrtle, flower gardens, lawns, along railroad tracks with dead elms, old fence rows with dead elms, rocks and vines, old abandoned foundations, and cedar swampy areas.

When you are hunting the white or caramel morels around dead red elms, the bulk of the find will be on the east and the north sides of the trees with some scattered around the west and south sides. Whites will grow by themselves and in groups, sometimes over very large areas.

If there are tall grasses near or next to dead elm trees, be especially careful because the morels love to grow in this type of grass. This is where your walking stick comes in very handy. What you want to do is go up to the tree carefully using your stick in front of you to part the grasses. You may get lucky and find some morels while slowly approaching the tree. A good tip to remember is that morels can be found from the base of the tree out to the edge of the tree's canopy.

Another good area to look for whites is around fruit trees, especially the apple tree. Look around the area of the apple tree where most of the growth is.

Another odd area to find whites is in a pasture frequented by cows and horses; the manure piles sometimes produce mushrooms. If you are hunting morels in a cattle pasture beware of any bulls. You are asking to get chased down by this large animal.

The following pictures give perspective on the variety of morel mushroom sizes.

A mushroom hunting buddy holding
a huge white morel mushroom.

PHOTO COURTESY OF RICHARD BURDICK

This picture shows the different sizes and shapes of white and gray morel mushrooms. In the background these morel mushrooms are bigger than the beverage can.

This picture shows a large plastic Tupperware pie container full of morel mushrooms. In the background a cigarette pack shows the comparative size of the mushrooms.

MOREL MUSHROOM CYCLE

For years, I was led to believe that there was a certain way to pick a morel mushroom, protecting the root system, which is truly a false understanding. There is no proper way to pick a mushroom, and there is no gigantic root system believed by many to protect hot spots. If you find a grouping of morels in an area, leave some of the smaller ones behind so they can dry and the spores can renew their cycle. Over picking will make areas unable to generate new mushrooms for coming years.

The spores of morel mushrooms are in the top two-thirds of the body. As the mushrooms dry out, the spores fall out, the germination process starts like a spider web of branching filaments (like mold on bread) under the leaves and can lay dormant for long periods of time (winter). In the spring the web of filaments continue to grow under the right conditions into a fruiting body. When the conditions are exactly right, the stem starts to grow which allows the mushroom to stand up.

OVER PICKING

When over picking happens, all the morel mushrooms in an area have been picked and none are left to decompose and spread their spores. If there are no morels left to decompose, there is little chance of finding mushrooms in these areas the following season. I used to be as guilty as anyone else for this, because I was always looking for every last mushroom in any given area.

About five years ago, I finally figured out what was happening to the areas where I used to find many morels and now was only finding a few. If you do not leave a few morels behind in these areas, your chances of finding any morels in the same location is going to decrease dramatically. Also if you are not the only person hunting in these areas, it is hard to leave some behind because someone else is likely to find the few you left for future growth.

To help solve this problem, take one or two of your mushrooms out of your bag and demolish them so nothing is left resembling a mushroom, and scatter this debris around to promote growth for future years of hunting. If you do not do this, your hunting areas will disappear simply due to greed. I know this is very hard to do because they are, at times, so hard to find, especially areas where morels were once found in abundance and now you might find a few or maybe none at all.

By doing this I have seen areas produce more morels than I could have thought to see again. This procedure works pretty well. Typically, the morel takes times to break down to spread its spores around. By breaking them apart, you speed up the cycle a little bit. The morel bits and pieces that you leave behind will dry out quicker, and no one but you will ever know. Other people won't realize there were mushrooms in the area when they cannot find any, and they probably will not even come back in the future.

FAIRY RINGS

A fairy ring is a partial circle which can be a small to large area covered with morel mushrooms. The very first one I ever found was an exceptionally huge area. It started out with 2–3" tall whites in the ring, and when I looked past the ring, the whites had grown 4–8" tall. There were about 40 morels in this one location.

Over the years I have found several of these fairy rings with all of the primary colors (blacks, grays, and whites). The black morel fairy rings were somewhat smaller, but the results were the same. The smaller blacks grew in the area of the partial circle. While looking for them, I would look past the initial edge to find where the bigger ones were so that I wouldn't accidently step on any while picking them.

I learned over time to mark the area where I first noticed the ring, either by using my walking staff or my backpack. I would leave something behind so I could look around thoroughly and make sure that I had gotten them all.

With each of the different groups of morel mushrooms, the fairy rings get progressively bigger. It is not uncommon to find more than one or two of these fairy rings in really good morel hunting areas where you may have found large quantities in the past.

TYPES OF TREES

There is a wide range of trees to look around and near, as well as man-made structures. The common types of trees are as follows: ash, aspen, beech, cedar, common choke cherry, dogwood, red and white elm, hemlock, hickory, lilac, maple, goosefoot maple (also known as a striped maple or moosewood), oaks, poplar, various types of pine, spruce, balsam fir, and fruit trees such as apple, pear, and peach.

Ash

The most common type of tree to look for when mushroom hunting is the ash tree. Get used to identifying trees by looking at the bark, because the leaves only start showing up toward the end of the black season and the beginning of the grays. The bark has an interesting diamond appearance and is gray to brown in color. The ash tree is commonly found from the eastern half of the US and as far west as Minnesota and Texas.

Common Choke Cherry

Another type of tree where you will find morels is the common choke cherry. The bark on a mature choke cherry is unique because it has a flaky appearance and is dark black in color.

Aspen

Another common tree for finding morels is the large tooth aspen, more commonly called the poplar or popple.

Below is a stand of young aspen, in an area which was part of a big logging operation fifteen to twenty years ago.

Beech

Beech trees are usually found in woods where morel mushrooms will grow. The younger ones keep their leaves until early spring. In the picture below there is one mature beech and a large area of young saplings.

Apple

This next picture is an apple tree. The apple tree is distinctly different when it comes to finding the morel mushroom. First, look at the tree's branches to find the most amount of growth. If the tree looks lopsided, then this is the area to look for all varieties of the morel. Remember that you will not find mushrooms growing around or under every tree. Morel mushrooms will only grow under apple trees if the soil content and weather conditions are right.

Elm

The elm tree is a great discovery when you are hunting white morels. When you find these trees, start looking around the base and out to the edge of the canopy.

A dead elm tree

The bark will have a splotchy look about it, meaning that the bark is already showing signs it is starting to fall off the tree. This usually begins near the top in the smaller branches and over time will work its way down the tree.

Bark of a dead elm

Some mushroom hunters, including myself, like to go into areas recently logged, either totally (clear cut) or partially (thinned out). Walking in these areas can be very challenging because you will be walking on and around leftover brush, stumps, and discarded log parts. I like newly logged areas because the loggers bring in big machinery to cut the trees down and drag them out which is known as skidding. When the loggers are doing this, they are moving and digging the soil up, making it look like a big disaster zone. For about a year or two I hunted these areas, especially around the stumps. Shortly after this time period, it becomes tough walking through the area because the prickers and briars appear. Once the new trees get big enough to shade them the briars can't grow.

The area above is known as a staging area; piles of different types of trees are stacked separately. Most of the time people won't see this part of the operation as it is done during the winter months. Sometimes they will harvest trees during other times of the year; however, I believe the loggers prefer to cut the trees down when the sap isn't in them. The following picture shows what the woods look like after the loggers leave.

RAILROAD TRACKS

Railroad tracks and railroad grades are very good places for hunting morel mushrooms. Whether you are hunting along tracks or old grades where the tracks are removed and abandoned, both are great areas to hunt. I like these kinds of areas for the white morels. For some reason the American elm likes to grow along these areas. When the American elms die or are killed by the crews who have to keep the trees away from the tracks, these dead elms are known for having white morels grow around them. On the old abandoned grades, these elms grow up and die off all the time. If there are railroad tracks in the area where you like to hunt, look up and down the tracks to see if there are any dead elms nearby.

Dead white elm next to railroad tracks.

MAN-MADE STRUCTURES

Man-made structures such as old foundations, stone walls, fence rows, graveyards, and current or abandoned railroad tracks are excellent places to hunt for morel mushrooms. With the exception of the railroad tracks, you can find all the different colors of morels in and around these unusual areas. Most of the time you will find the whites, especially if there is a dead elm tree mixed in with them.

Morel growing next to a concrete step

The biggest black morel mushrooms I ever found were growing next to an old stone wall with vines growing over it. The mushrooms were found on the east and north sides of the wall, because these were cool and damp areas where the midday and afternoon sun could not dry out the area.

GAME ANIMALS

Over the years of hunting morel mushrooms, I have found morels growing in really odd places away from any particular tree groups where they would normally grow. When the spores of the morels that are not picked finally get released into the air to float off to their new growing locations for the next season, some land right where they were growing while others get blown away and may land on grasses or other plants. These plants are sometimes eaten by rabbits and other animals. As these animals move around from area to area their droppings release what they have eaten back into nature. I have found morel mushrooms growing in these droppings. I have also found them growing around brush piles where rabbits are frequently found.

Finding morels this way even occurs with white-tailed deer, mule deer, and elk. When they travel from one area to another, they use trails from their bedding area to their eating area. Big game hunters call these trails "runs." These runs are the same areas where the bigger game animals leave their fecal droppings. I have found morel mushrooms growing along these runs, sometimes right in the droppings.

PROCESSING YOUR MOREL MUSHROOMS

When you get back home you will want to take care of and preserve all the morel mushrooms found that day. The first thing I do is to take my big wash container out. Based on the size and quantity of morels I found, I may use either a small plastic container set aside for my mushrooms or the 40-gallon plastic barrel that I cut down to work as a bigger wash basin.

The next step is to fill the container with cold water. I get my mushroom bag out and carefully place the morels into the cold water. Then I gently rub the mushrooms with both hands to clean them of sand and any bugs or worms that may be on them.

Some mushroom hunters mix salt into the water to clean the morels as a shortcut to kill bugs and slugs; however, this is a process I avoid for two reasons. First, salt changes the flavor of the morels. Second, when I slice the morels I am able to remove any bugs at that time.

From this point forward I have a table set up near the washing area to sort out the different colors of the morel mushrooms and put them in separate one-quart containers to be sold to the people who don't choose to go out and find their own. The average one-quart container is about one pound and the mushrooms are usually sold by the pound. I very rarely sell mine because I give them away to friends who can no longer get into the woods to find their own.

After washing the morels, I take both hands and gently lift the morels out and shake them to get most of the water off. Next, I put them on a cutting board close by and use a filet knife to slice the morels in half lengthwise. Depending on the size of the mushroom, they can be sliced into smaller sections. During this part I always look for bugs or slugs on the inner side of the mushroom. I use the tip of the knife to remove them and put them in a separate bowl. I place the sliced mushrooms into a colander. Once all of the cleaning is done, I take the junk bowl and the water container out into the yard or garden and dump the contents in a chosen spot every time I clean mushrooms.

Next it is time to decide how many mushrooms will be eaten right away and how many should be saved for later. After deciding, the next step is to get a good-size storage container with a push down lid or a vacuum-vented lid and some paper towels. Take enough paper towel to put a single layer in the bottom of the storage container and moisten the towel with water, but don't get it dripping wet.

Start placing the morels in a single layer on the paper towel. Don't pile the mushrooms on each other; you want the edges touching the paper towels. Once there is a layer of mushrooms in the container, place another layer of moistened paper towels on top and start another layer. Continue doing this procedure until all of the mushrooms which are going to be eaten in the upcoming week are in the container. Place the storage container in a refrigerator to keep it cool until you are ready to cook them.

Earlier I mentioned a storage procedure known as drying. Drying is necessary process to preserve the morels and is done in three different ways as noted below. Choose the one that works best for you.

1. Screens: Place the morels on screens on some kind of a stand. I put them in an area where the wind cannot get to them.
2. Strings: Put the morels on strings with a needle and thread without letting the mushrooms touch each other. When you get a string of mushrooms to a desirable length, tie it off with a loop on both ends so they can be hung up to dry.
3. Dehydrator: The third and final way to dry morels is in a dehydrator. I don't like this method because it dries them too much. If you choose this procedure, you can purchase your own dehydrator at a store in your area. Prices vary from around thirty dollars for a low-end dehydrator to several hundred dollars for a high-end model.

After the morels have dried, transfer them to either storage bags or storage containers to protect them from getting damaged. I group them into serving-size portions and put them in storage bags, getting as much air out as possible without hurting them. Then I put the bags in the storage containers. I double protect them in case the storage container gets damaged, cracked, or broken to prevent the bagged mushrooms from becoming wet or spilled.

The next few pictures show morel mushrooms being rinsed off in a sink of cold water and then being moved to a temporary drying area to be prepared for a feast.

Rinsing the mushrooms in the sink

Temporary drying area

The next three pictures show morel mushrooms after they have been rinsed and sliced in preparation for the drying process. Here we use screens for the drying. The pictures show the morels lying on a screen before they are put outside to dry. It's best to wait for a day when there is no wind to blow the morels off the screens.

PHOTO COURTESY OF RICHARD BURDICK

Drying area

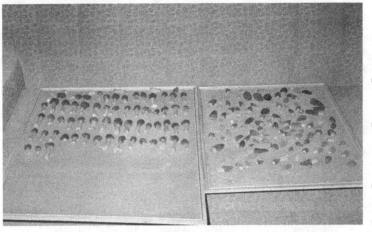

Screen to dry the mushrooms inside

*My friend Steve Morse, with screens of mushrooms
outside to continue the drying process*

JOURNALS

Journals can be useful when it comes to mushroom hunting. Here are some helpful things to put in a journal:

1. Date – Always put the date of your hunt.
2. Weather conditions – The mushroom season is about six to eight weeks long. If the weather conditions switch and make a sudden change from cool and warm to hot for an extended period of time this will put an end to the season very quickly. Keeping track of the weather is very important.
3. Good spots – Recording the places that you have hunted and found mushrooms is important. Also record which types of morels were found in each location.
4. Bad spots – You may have found an area that looks great, but never find any mushrooms. It is important to note this in your journal as a place to never return. Also note in the journal locations of clay, because you won't find any morels in these areas.
5. Trees and grasses – Keep track of the soil contents, various grasses and trees, and other information about the location.

MUSHROOMER'S LOG

Date	Weather	Location		Trees/ Grasses
			◊ Good ◊ Bad	
			◊ Good ◊ Bad	
			◊ Good ◊ Bad	
			◊ Good ◊ Bad	
			◊ Good ◊ Bad	
			◊ Good ◊ Bad	
			◊ Good ◊ Bad	
			◊ Good ◊ Bad	
			◊ Good ◊ Bad	
			◊ Good ◊ Bad	
			◊ Good ◊ Bad	
			◊ Good ◊ Bad	
			◊ Good ◊ Bad	
			◊ Good ◊ Bad	
			◊ Good ◊ Bad	
			◊ Good ◊ Bad	

Date	Weather	Location		Trees/ Grasses
			◊ Good ◊ Bad	
			◊ Good ◊ Bad	
			◊ Good ◊ Bad	
			◊ Good ◊ Bad	
			◊ Good ◊ Bad	
			◊ Good ◊ Bad	
			◊ Good ◊ Bad	
			◊ Good ◊ Bad	
			◊ Good ◊ Bad	
			◊ Good ◊ Bad	
			◊ Good ◊ Bad	
			◊ Good ◊ Bad	
			◊ Good ◊ Bad	
			◊ Good ◊ Bad	
			◊ Good ◊ Bad	
			◊ Good ◊ Bad	
			◊ Good ◊ Bad	
			◊ Good ◊ Bad	

RECIPES

Biscuits and Morel Gravy

Courtesy of Reggie, in Iowa

Ingredients:

Morel mushrooms
Flour
Cooking grease
Milk
Salt and pepper

Directions:

Slice, soak and rinse your morels as you would in any normal preparation.
Lightly flour the morels and fry in cooking grease until fully cooked.
Add flour to the grease to dry it up, continually stirring.
Slowly add milk, stirring until it's the texture you desire.
Salt and pepper to taste.
Pour over biscuits!

Breakfast Morels

Courtesy of Moses

Ingredients:

Dried morel mushrooms
Milk
Eggs
Cheese
Salt and pepper

Directions:

Crumble up dried morels.
Soak in just a little milk for approximately 1 hour.
Add mixture to eggs and scramble.
Add cheese, salt and pepper to taste.

Morels and Asparagus

Courtesy of Susan

Ingredients:

Morels fried in lots of butter, salt and pepper to taste
Fresh Asparagus tips, cooked until tender
Crisp fried bacon slices
Poached eggs
Hollandaise sauce

Directions:

On a plate, arrange ingredients in order as listed below:
1. Fresh cooked asparagus tips
2. Fried morels in butter
3. Crisp bacon slices
4. Two poached eggs
5. Cover with lots of Hollandaise Sauce

Morel and Bacon Appetizers

Courtesy of Todd
Near Mt. Adams, Washington

Ingredients:

Morel mushrooms the size of your thumb or larger
Maple-cured bacon
Brown sugar
Toothpicks

Directions:

Wrap morels with bacon. Pin with a toothpick.
Place wrapped morels on a cookie sheet and broil until bacon is done. Turn at least once to ensure the bacon is fully cooked. When done, remove from oven and sprinkle with brown sugar.

Morels and Nachos

Courtesy of Larry

Ingredients:

Butter
Onion
Seasoned salt
Garlic powder
Ground pepper
Nacho chips
Cheese
Tomatoes
Scallions
Chilies
Olives

Directions:

Sauté onion in butter.
Season with seasoned salt, a bit of garlic powder, and fresh ground pepper.
Place nacho chips in a large 12" x 18" cake pan and cover with your favorite cheese.
Bake at 350 degrees until the cheese is melted and the chips are warmed.
Toss a liberal amount of morels into the fry pan with the onions.
Enjoy the heavenly aroma whilst cooking.
When done, drain excess butter from the frying pan.
Dump the mushrooms and onion mix in with the nachos.
Add tomatoes, scallions, chilies, and olives.
Dig in!

Breading, Oil and Garlic...

Courtesy of Steve and Carla G

Ingredients:

Morel mushrooms
Milk
Flour
Cornmeal
Salt and pepper or seasoned salt
Olive or Canola oil
Minced garlic or shallots

Directions:

Soak morel mushrooms in milk to coat.
Roll morels in a mixture of half flour/half cornmeal.
Add salt/pepper or seasoned salt to taste.
Heat olive or canola oil in a skillet.
Add breaded morels to skillet with minced garlic or shallots.

Serve as a side dish, or on top of steak.

Drakes Batter Mix Recipe

Courtesy of the author

Ingredients:

1 empty paper lunch bag (preferably a new one)
2 cups washed and sliced morel mushrooms
1-½ cups Drakes batter mix (http://drakesbattermix.com)
¼ cup butter or olive oil

Directions:

Put ¾ cup Drakes into the bag.
Place half of the morels into the bag.
Close the bag (folding it over twice) and shake the bag firmly several times. Set aside.
Melt half of the butter in a medium-sized skillet using a wooden spoon to stir.
Remove morels from bag and place them in the skillet.
Cook until golden brown, flip the mushrooms over and cook until golden brown on the other side.
Remove morels from skillet and place on a pre-warmed plate.
Cover with a paper towel and set aside.
Repeat process for the rest of the morels. They are great as is or as a side dish.

Variant: Deep fry morels in olive oil

Transfer morels from the bag (step 1 from above) to the fryer basket.
Deep fry for about 30 seconds. Using the utensil that came with the fryer, push down on the mushrooms a few times.
Remove basket and place cooked mushrooms on a pre-warmed plate.
Cover with a paper towel and set aside.
Repeat the processes with the remaining Drakes batter mix and mushrooms.
This process using the olive oil is great for those who can't have butter.

Morels And Beer....That's Right, Beer!

Courtesy of Scott
Door County, WI

Ingredients:

Salt water
Hunk of butter
2 splashes Heineken Beer
Seasoned salt
Hot sauce

Directions:

Soak mushrooms in salt water then cut in halves.

Heat a cast iron skillet (still available at Farm & Fleet) with a huge hunk of butter.

Throw the mushrooms in the skillet.

Add a couple splashes of beer (probably from the bottle you are drinking in celebration of your find, but Heineken is best).

Sprinkle with seasoning salts and a bit of hot sauce. Cover.

Turn and stir mushrooms occasionally (and don't forget to drink your victory beer, too).

Cook for 20 minutes or so on medium heat.

Serve with anything and enjoy!

Simple Recipe with Corn Flakes

Courtesy of Doughboy

Ingredients:

Morels
Butter
2-3 eggs (depending on the batch)
Kellogg's Corn Flakes, crumbled
Salt

Directions:

Whisk eggs in bowl until well mixed.
Fill another bowl with Corn Flake crumbs.
Add a pinch of salt if desired.
Dip morels in egg mixture.
Lightly coat morels on both sides with cereal crumbs.
Fry in lots of butter and flip when light brown.
Add more butter if necessary until done.

Simple Recipe with Potato Chips

Courtesy of Becky W.
Ohio

Ingredients:

Morels
1 stick of butter
1 bag of potato chips, crumbled
Garlic salt to taste

Directions:

Melt butter in a heavy skillet.
Dip morels in melted butter, then roll in potato chip crumbs.
Fry until golden brown.
Top with sprinkle of garlic salt.

A Grandmother's Morel Recipe

Courtesy of Laurie L.

Ingredients:

One batch of morels
1 egg
¼ cup milk
1 cup cornmeal
1 teaspoon black pepper
Bacon grease

Directions:

Clean and halve the morels then soak "a while" or overnight in salt water, using a heavy plate to weigh them down. At cooking time, rinse well and drain the morels.

In a wide shallow bowl mix egg and milk. Set aside.

Combine cornmeal and black pepper in a thick paper bag. Set aside

Using a deep well-seasoned cast iron skillet, melt bacon grease 1" deep. Get it good and hot but not smoking.

Dip mushrooms in egg and milk mixture, and let soak while the grease is heating.

Take a handful out of the bowl and shake slightly to get off excess liquid.

Drop mushrooms into bag of cornmeal.

Hold the bottom of the bag so it doesn't break, and gently shake. Add more mushrooms, shaking after each addition.

When all are coated well, lay a single layer of mushrooms in the hot skillet.

Try to only turn them once, so the coating stays on better.

Don't salt; bacon grease is already salty.

When golden, drain and paper. Or, gently dump the coated morels in a colander set in a larger bowl. This lets the loose stuff fall off and if you need to touch up any bare spots your coating is right there.

My husband's family uses cracker crumbs and they made a production line out it for extra family fun.

Morels and Asparagus

Courtesy of Nils F.

Spring morels and fresh spring asparagus, the two are a marriage made in heaven.

Ingredients:

Butter
Morel mushrooms
Asparagus
Garlic

Directions:

Slice morels, asparagus, and garlic.
Boil asparagus until tender.
Sauté mushrooms in the butter and garlic.
Add the asparagus and sauté until asparagus is done.
Throw it on a plate, splash with a bit of lemon and fresh cracked pepper.

That's it. It's truly the best you will ever encounter.

Sweet and Salty Morels

Courtesy of anonymous in the Village of Stratton

Ingredients:

Morel mushrooms
Flour
Seasoning (garlic and pepper)
Diet Coke
Crackers

Directions:

Coat morels mushrooms with flour and place in frying pan.
Season to taste.
Pour Diet Coke into frying pan.
Cook for 10-15 minutes.

Serve with crackers.
The mushrooms are sweet from the pop, and eating them with crackers adds the salty taste. Yum!

Broccoli Mushroom Cheddar Cheese Soup

Ingredients:

2 (10 oz.) packages frozen chopped broccoli
3 ½ cups chicken broth, divided
10 large mushrooms, sliced
⅔ cup finely chopped celery
⅓ cup chopped green onion
1 tablespoon finely chopped parsley
2 tablespoons butter
2 teaspoons garlic salt
1½ cups grated mild cheddar cheese
½ cup sour cream
½ teaspoon Tabasco

Directions:

Cook broccoli as directed on package. Drain.
Puree broccoli in blender with 1 ½ cups chicken broth.
Simmer pureed broccoli mixture in remaining broth.
In a separate pan, sauté celery, onions, and mushrooms until the onions are transparent.
Season vegetables with garlic salt and parsley.
Add pureed broccoli. Cover and cook over low heat for 30 minutes.
Stir in grated cheese, sour cream, and Tabasco.
Serve after the cheese has melted. Serves 6.

Cream Of Morel Soup

Courtesy of David H. - Located in Petoskey, MI
A heavenly soup that will make you want to get back to the
woods and feed more black flies.

Ingredients:

¾ lb. fresh morels (more or less to taste), chopped
1 large leek (use everything below the green leaves)
3 medium to small russet potatoes, peeled and halved
1 cup chicken stock
1 cup heavy cream
½ dry white wine
2 tablespoons butter
Salt and pepper to taste
2 cups water

Directions:

Chop off dark green leek leaves and roots. Slice the stem
lengthwise and rinse under cold water making sure to remove
all the grit trapped between layers.
Add leeks and potatoes to soup pot with 2 cups water.
Boil moderately until quite tender, 20-30 minutes.
In a medium pan over medium flame, add butter, morels and a
few dashes of salt.
Cook morels gently for 15 minutes, making sure they don't dry
out. Add a few dashes of wine at a time to keep moist.
When nearly done, add wine, turn up flame and continue
cooking until liquid is almost gone.
Add chicken stock and stir until blended.
When potatoes and leeks are tender, remove from heat and
blend until smooth. Return to pot.
Add morel mix to potato/leek mixture and simmer very gently,
stirring occasionally to avoid scorching. After about 5-10
minutes, add cream, salt and pepper to taste.

Minnesota Wild Rice Mushroom Soup

Ingredients:

⅓ cup wild rice, cooked
¼ cup butter
1 small onion
12 oz. package of fresh mushrooms
¼ cup flour
2 cups chicken broth
2 cups half & half (or 2 tablespoons butter with 1¾ cups milk)
Water chestnuts, carrots, and celery (optional)

Directions:

Melt butter in saucepan
Gradually stir in flour and half & half.
Cook, stirring continuously, until soup base thickens.
In a separate pan, brown onion and sliced mushrooms.
Add cooked wild rice to vegetables.
Stir entire mixture in soup base and serve.

Morel Mushroom Soup

Ingredients:

4 cups fresh morels
1 medium onion, chopped
2 stalks celery, chopped
2 cups asparagus, cooked
1 tablespoon oil
4 cups milk
4 tablespoons whole wheat flour
Salt and pepper to taste

Directions:

Sauté morels, onion, and celery in oil until slightly tender.
Gradually stir in flour; then add milk, salt, and pepper.
Add cooked asparagus.
Simmer until thickened.

Wild Mushrooms And Rice

Ingredients:

3 cups morel mushrooms, sliced
2 tablespoons butter
1 tablespoon all purpose flour
¼ teaspoon cinnamon
1 (10 ¼ oz.) can chicken broth
Hot cooked rice

Directions:

Over medium heat, melt butter then add mushrooms and sauté
until tender.
Stir in flour and cinnamon.
Cook, stirring continuously, until mixture is thick and bubbly.
Stir in chicken broth and bring sauce to a boil while stirring.
Let boil for an additional minute.
Remove from heat and spoon sauce over cooked rice.
Serves 4.

Angel Morels

Courtesy of Diahnn
Illinois

Ingredients:

1/3 cup diced onion (Vidalia preferred)
4 tablespoons butter
1/3 cup diced green onion and red pepper
1 pound fresh morels, sliced in half vertically
2 tablespoon flour
1 teaspoon salt
1 teaspoon sugar
1 tablespoon soy sauce
½ lb. of angel hair pasta

Directions:

Prepare pasta according to directions and drain.

In a large sauté pan, sauté pepper and onion in 2 tablespoons butter for 1 minute.

Make a roux out of the flour, soy sauce, salt, and sugar in a separate pan (it has to be stirred constantly).

Turn the heat to low then add the morels, onion, and red pepper mixture.

Cover and cook 30 minutes.

Pour morel sauce over pasta and serve.

Medallions Of Beef Forestiere

Ingredients:

6 – ¼ lb. slices beef tenderloin
Salt and pepper to taste
2 tablespoons butter
2 tablespoons finely chopped shallots
1 teaspoon finely chopped garlic
6 oz. fresh mushrooms, thinly sliced (oyster, shiitake, or morels, if possible)
1 cup beef or veal broth
½ cup dry red wine, preferably Zinfandel
¼ cup Madeira wine (1 substitute Vermouth)
4 tablespoons butter, at room temp.

Directions:

Sprinkle salt and pepper over beef.
In saucepan, melt 1 tablespoon butter.
Add shallots and garlic. Stir, cooking briefly.
Add sliced mushrooms. Stirring constantly, cook for about 3 minutes.
Add ¼ cup dry red wine and stir. Cook until reduced by half.
Add beef or veal broth.
Bring sauce to a boil then add remaining dry red wine and the Madeira wine.
Cook and reduce to approximately 1¼ cups.
Heat 1 tablespoon butter in a heavy skillet and add tenderloin slices.
Cook meat on each side for 2-3 minutes or until brown.
Transfer meat to warm platter.
Add mushroom sauce to skillet. Stir and dissolve the brown tidbits clinging to the pan.
Swirl 4 tablespoons butter into sauce.
Spoon over cooked tenderloins and serve.

Morel Shish Kabobs

Courtesy of Jeff R.

Ingredients:

Medium to large morel mushrooms
Bacon Grease
Parsley
Green onion
Chopped walnuts

Directions:

Rinse the morels mushrooms and pat dry.
Stuff morels with a mixture of the bacon grease, parsley, green onion, and chopped walnuts.
Line 3 to 4 stuffed mushrooms on a kabob skewer.
Place skewers low over hot coals and rotate frequently.
The bacon grease will fry the inside mixture while the outside morel get crunchy.

Spring Morels & Pork in an Entrée

Ingredients:

For two people, you will need:
1 pound pork cutlets cut very thin
2 cups morel mushrooms
¼ cup butter
¼ cup dry white wine
1 cup of your favorite brown sauce
Salt and pepper

Directions:

Trim the fat off the pork cutlets and pound them out.
Melt butter in a sauté pan.
Add the cutlets and mushrooms. Sauté two minutes.
Add white wine and cook for thirty seconds.
Add the brown sauce and finish with a little butter.

Serve with a Michigan wine that has a slight hint of sweetness. Try the Chateau Grand Traverse Dry Riesling. It's a marriage made in heaven.

Morels in Sweet Red Wine

Courtesy of Debby & Ken
Near Porter Corners, NY

Ingredients:

10 hand-sized morels
½ cup of butter
½ cup sweet red wine
1 cup warm water
¼ cup flour
½ teaspoon salt
½ teaspoon fresh pepper
1 teaspoon garlic, chopped fine

Directions:

Slowly add warm water to the flour, stirring until all the water is completely combined, with no lumps.
Add salt and pepper.
Slice the morels in quarters.
Dry thoroughly.
Fry morels in butter and garlic until tender.
When tender, take out the mushrooms.
Now all the water the mushrooms released is in the pan. Reduce the stock until thick.
Turn the heat to high. When the stock is boiling hard, quickly add the red wine, stirring to loosen any morel bits that may have stuck to the pan.
Lower the heat and, once again, reduce the stock.
Add the flour/water mixture and stir until thick.
Pour thickened sauce onto the cooked morels.

Morels in Wine Sauce

Ingredients:

Oil
Butter
Scallions
Garlic
Dehydrated morels
White wine
Fresh parsley
Ground pepper
Toast

Directions:

Heat a combination of oil and butter in a pan.
Add scallions and/or garlic with dehydrated morels.
Gently sauté, until morels are lightly browned and have absorbed the butter and oil.
Remove the morels and deglaze pan with white wine.
Reduce by half, and then return morels with freshly chopped parsley.
Simmer a few minutes.
Serve on toast with freshly ground pepper.

Olive Oil and Garlic

Courtesy of Carla G.

The all-time morel recipe in our family.

Ingredients:

Morel Mushrooms
Pure olive oil
Fresh garlic
Marsala Wine

Directions:

Take your "find of the day," and sauté the morels in pure olive oil, fresh garlic, and a little Marsala Wine.

Very scrumptious!

FREEZER STORAGE

Lock In The Flavor Before You Freeze

Ingredients and supplies:
Morel Mushrooms
1 lunch size paper bag
1 cup Drake's Batter Mix
¼ cup butter (for pan frying only)
1 Teflon baking sheet

Directions:
1. Clean morels.
2. Open lunch bag so it can stand by itself.
3. Put Drake's batter mix into the bag.
4. Add about 1 big handful of morels.
5. Close the bag and using both hands (one hand on top, keeping the bag closed and the other hand supporting the bag's bottom side) shake the bag firmly up and down a few times.

Directions for partial pan frying in butter:
Cook morels halfway and flip over once.
Remove from pan and place on baking sheet. Do not let any of the morels touch each other. Being careful, put this sheet into the freezer until morels are frozen.
Remove the sheet with frozen half-cooked morels from freezer. Put morels in meal proportions into Ziploc bags. To protect the bags in the freezer, put into a sealable storage container.

Directions for partial baking:

Preheat oven to 375°F.

Follow steps 1 – 5 above.

Place morels onto an ungreased non-stick baking sheet. Do not let any morels touch each other.

Bake for 15 minutes.

Remove the sheet from oven and put directly into freezer until mushrooms are frozen.

Put the morels in meal proportions in Ziploc bags. To protect bags in the freezer, put bags into a sealable storage container.

When you decide to have a meal of morels, remove the bags from the freezer and finish cooking them.

Enjoy!

INDEX

ABOUT THE AUTHOR

MICHAEL E. PHILLIPS

As I was growing up, there were some roads I am glad I went down. While in high school I studied earth sciences, horticultural sciences, and a lot of art classes. Today I think the art classes I took have helped me with my passion for the outdoors, because I now design and build beautiful and extremely detailed wildlife and nature scenes out of stained glass.

In the sciences I have a deep passion for flowers and the flowers of weeds. In college I studied dendrology and fisheries, and it was during this time that I was introduced to morel mushrooming. With all of the sciences that I studied, I especially use the dendrology while walking in the woods or just driving around different areas. I catch myself looking for certain types of trees. When I find these specific types of trees, I take time to make a note of them and their location.

Just recently I have given up on keeping mental notes and I am using a hand-held recorder so I don't have to remember the specific particulars about future morel mushrooming areas of interest. It started about 25 years ago when there wasn't a day that would go by that I would not be thinking about the next morel mushroom season. With me, morel mushrooming had become an obsession. If I wasn't driving or walking to seek out new areas, I would be deep in thought about a fabulous stained glass window pattern of morel mushrooms in the wild and with wildlife included.

I have no regrets about my research and observation with the morel mushroom, and I can hardly wait for the next season to come.